THE HUNTINGTON

LIBRARY • ART COLLECTIONS • BOTANICAL GARDENS

TEXT PREPARED BY PEGGY PARK BERNAL

HUNTINGTON LIBRARY
SAN MARINO, CALIFORNIA

The Huntington

Library • Art Collections • Botanical Gardens
1151 Oxford Road   San Marino, California   91108

General Information: (818) 405-2141
Membership Information: (818) 405-2290
Business Offices: (818) 405-2100

Huntington Library Museum Publications Committee
Guilland Sutherland   *Hubert Kozak*

PHOTOGRAPHIC CREDITS

Kit Amorn: title page detail, introduction pages 12-13, 14 (bottom), 17 (bottom), 18, 19 (top), 20 (top), 21, 23 (top), 24 (bottom), 26 (bottom), 27 (middle, bottom), front flap (top), back cover
Don Milici: title page
Kathlene Persoff: cover, front flap (bottom), pages 17 (top), 22, 29, 44 (top)

Don Normark: pages 25 (top), 28
Saxon Holt: pages 14 (top), 15
Melba Levick: page 24 (top)
John N. Trager: pages 20 (bottom), 26 (top)
Clair Martin: page 16
Bob Schlosser: inside front cover, pages 19 (bottom), 23 (bottom), 29 (bottom), 50-51
Jerry Fredrick: page 63
Sculpture (back cover) of *Diana,* by

Anna Hyatt Huntington, lent by the Fogg Art Museum, Harvard University, gift of Mr. and Mrs. Archer M. Huntington

Historical photographs from Huntington archives. All photographs of the art and library collections by Bob Schlosser and John Sullivan, Huntington photography department.

PRODUCED BY

Legacy Publishing   2020 Alameda Padre Serra   Santa Barbara, CA 93103
Project Manager: *Cynthia Anderson*   Designer: *Dianne Elliott*   Production: *Nancy M. Swanson*
Managing Editor: *Courtney C. Fischer*

CONTENTS

Introduction

 ew places in the world, if any, offer the combination of treasures for both visitors and scholars that the Huntington does. The 130-acre Botanical Gardens feature specialized areas for roses, palms, camellias, and herbs, as well as Japanese, subtropical, desert, and jungle plants. The Art Collections are distinguished by one of the most important collections in this country of British art of the late eighteenth and early nineteenth centuries, and by a small but fine collection of American paintings and decorative art. The Library has a rich collection of rare books, manuscripts, and photographs which spans ten centuries of history and literature in Britain and America.

The mission of the Huntington is to preserve and display these magnificent collections and to make them available to individuals engaged in scholarly research and other creative work in history, literature, art, and science. Information about the holdings is disseminated through exhibitions, lectures, classes, and publications.

Each year more than half a million people of all ages visit the Huntington. In addition, every year nearly 2,000 scholars (called "readers") work with the collections in their efforts to advance learning through research. An increasing number receive fellowships from the Huntington to make their studies possible. The Huntington publishes a scholarly journal, catalogs, bibliographies, facsimiles, and guides; it is one of the oldest book publishers in Southern California.

A private, non-profit institution, the Huntington is governed by a five-member Board of Trustees, assisted by a Board of Overseers — all leading private citizens who volunteer their time. H. E. Huntington left an endowment to provide operating income for the institution, but the endowment income now supplies less than two-thirds of the amount needed each year. All the rest must be provided by individual, foundation, and corporate donations.

7

A distant view of the rose garden and its tempietto, across the south terrace of the Huntington Gallery.

The Huntington residence, c. 1920.

The San Marino Ranch

Today San Marino, California, is known throughout the world as the location of the Huntington, with its unique botanical gardens, its art gallery of masterpieces, and its famous library. Yet before 1920, to most people "San Marino" meant the tiny republic between Forli and Pesaro in Italy. The name was planted in California in 1877 when James De Barth Shorb and his wife Maria de Jesus Wilson christened their ranch San Marino in memory of Shorb's boyhood home in Maryland. His grandfather, it is said, had so named his estate because its acreage was identical to that of the Italian republic.

Here, in the spring of 1892, H. E. Huntington was entertained by the Shorbs. He was on a tour of Southern California in connection with railway business. The Shorb place, or rather its possibilities as a California home, stayed in his mind; he bought it ten years later.

The Huntingtons at Home

The home of Mr. and Mrs. Huntington, now the Art Gallery, was designed by Los Angeles architects Myron Hunt and Elmer Grey and built during the years 1909 to 1911. This handsome and spacious residence overlooking the San Gabriel Valley was first occupied by the Huntingtons in 1914. Its general style is Beaux Arts, adapted to the California climate and landscape.

The structure was very much as we know it today, except for the Main Exhibition Gallery, which replaced a service wing. The rooms on the ground floor functioned as their names suggest, and the art objects were an integral part of the living environment: the meals were served in the dining room, cards were played in one of the drawing rooms, and Mr. Huntington read in the library room amid the Louis XV furniture, with the Boucher tapestries on the walls around him.

The loggia of the Huntington residence in the 1920s.

Collis P. Huntington (left), newspaper boy, and Collis's nephew Henry E. Huntington (right) in San Francisco, c. 1892.

The second floor was used for bedrooms: Mr. Huntington occupied the room on the southeast corner in which conversation-piece portraits now hang, while Mrs. Huntington had an adjacent suite. The two secretaries, Mrs. Huntington's companion, and Mr. Huntington's valet had rooms on the second floor, and there was also space for guests. Frequent visitors included Sir Joseph Duveen (the principal source of art objects), Dr. A. S. W. Rosenbach (the principal source of manuscripts and rare books in Mr. Huntington's later years), and Homer L. Ferguson, the president of the Newport News Shipbuilding and Dry Dock Company, a Huntington enterprise.

The Huntingtons' life in San Marino was relatively simple. The estate offered a number of diversions which everyone could enjoy, such as the aviaries full of tropical birds and the croquet lawn on the North Vista. There was a billiard room, a bowling alley, a pitch-and-putt golf course, and plenty of gardens for walking. A moderate amount of entertaining took place, particularly of family. There were touches of elegance: only orange tree wood was used in the fireplaces, one dressed for dinner, and there were four footmen in attendance even when the Huntingtons dined alone. Cards were played afterwards, bridge if the group was sufficient, otherwise hearts. To the west, the Huntingtons' neighbor was George Patton, father of the World War II general. It is said that the small canyon between the two properties was used as the stake in the card games played by the two friends, a piece of land that changed hands as often as did their luck at cards.

Henry Edwards Huntington: Early Years

Henry Edwards Huntington was born in 1850 in Oneonta, New York. At the age of twenty, he moved to New York City, intent on making his own way. A year later he joined the railroad enterprises of his uncle, Collis P. Huntington, an association that lasted thirty years and ended at Collis's death in 1900.

Both men were railroad executives at the time of the westward expansion. In 1892, H. E. Huntington moved to San Francisco to share with his uncle the management of the Southern Pacific Company, a holding company for the Southern Pacific and Central Pacific railroads. In 1902, H. E. Huntington withdrew from the management of the Southern Pacific, moved to Los Angeles, and bought the San Marino Ranch. His family remained in San Francisco, and his first marriage ended in divorce a few years later.

9

Mr. Huntington in Los Angeles

Mr. Huntington had great faith in the potential of Southern California to become a major commercial and cultural center. He began immediately to put his plans into effect to develop the area. He organized the Los Angeles interurban railway system, the trains popularly

known as the Red Cars, which provided quick, efficient, and inexpensive transportation throughout the greater Los Angeles area. He acquired large tracts of land for urban and suburban development and built the electric power and distribution systems that were necessary to support future growth.

In 1910, at the age of sixty, Mr. Huntington sold much of his interest in his urban railway systems and began to devote most of his attention to books, his lifelong love, and to the growing collection which formed the nucleus of one of the great research libraries of the world.

Arabella Huntington, c. 1910.

10

The Mausoleum

The mausoleum of Henry Edwards and Arabella Huntington is, perhaps, the most beautiful building on the grounds. Constructed of Colorado Yule marble, it is located about a third of a mile northwest of the entrance pavilion on a high point of the property overlooking the gardens. It was a favorite location on the grounds for the Huntingtons and, in fact, the place chosen by Mrs. Huntington for her burial site.

Mr. Huntington selected John Russell Pope (1874-1937), one of America's most distinguished architects, to design the mausoleum in the form of a Greek temple. Pope used the classic circular peristyle (or double colonnade) "because it presented a perfect front from every angle, and furthermore it was a combination of two perfect forms, the circle and sphere." Pope later employed the same design in the construction of the Jefferson Memorial in Washington, D.C.

The Huntington memorial may be appreciated both as a graceful ornament to the gardens and as a solemn sepulcher. Four panels, sculpted by John Gregory, are mounted on masonry piers which alternate with the columns of the inner peristyle. The panels represent the four seasons and are inscribed with verses to represent the four stages of life.

Mr. Huntington's ambition was to build a preeminent research library which would concentrate on British and American history and literature. He bought manuscripts and rare books at a furious rate, frequently purchasing entire libraries, often at extremely high prices. He created a major collection in a few short years.

At the beginning, the books were kept in New York. As soon as his San Marino library building was completed in 1921, railroad cars full of books began to arrive in Southern California, where they were to be permanently housed.

While his book collections were growing, Mr. Huntington developed an interest in art, which he started collecting in 1907. He chose to specialize in British portraits of the eighteenth century. There can be little doubt that it was Arabella, widow of Collis Huntington, who urged him to enlarge his collecting activities to include art as well as books. She was one of the wealthiest women in America and, especially after Collis's death in 1900, one of the most important collectors of her generation.

Henry Edwards and Arabella Huntington were married in 1913 when they were both in their early sixties, and they collected art together until Arabella died in 1924. Until his own death three years later, Mr. Huntington continued to add to the art collection as a memorial to his wife.

Mr. Huntington laid careful plans for the use of his collections. In 1919 he founded a research institution to serve scholars. The deed of trust establishing guidelines for the Huntington institution allowed for growth and flexibility to meet changing conditions.

The Huntington Library, Art Collections, and Botanical Gardens are the contemporary embodiment of the founding indenture.

The Botanical Gardens

enry Edwards Huntington was by nature a builder—of railroads, of book and art collections, and of gardens. His inclination in all of his building was to specialize and to be satisfied with nothing less than first class. When he bought the 600-acre San Marino Ranch in 1903 it was a working ranch, with a sparse growth of native plants. In the early days, much of the land was given over to citrus cultivation; the remnants of the orchards may still be seen today, in the area between the mausoleum and the main parking lot. In 1904, he hired a young landscape gardener named William Hertrich, age twenty-six, and together they developed the grounds, slowly over a period of years. First came the lily ponds, the palm garden, and the desert collection, then the North Vista, the rose garden, the cycad collection, and the Japanese garden. About half of the acreage had been developed as gardens by 1927; the development of new lawns and gardens has been continuous ever since. Today, visitors can explore and enjoy fifteen different gardens containing about 14,000 different kinds of plants.

Mr. Huntington was always on the lookout for new things to grow. He saved avocado seed from the Jonathan Club, an exclusive gentlemen's club in Los Angeles, and that seed became an avocado grove, said to be the first commercial growth of avocados in California. He also saved the seed from melons he ate in France, and sent Hertrich horse chestnuts he picked up, the seed of mountain laurel and Spanish melons, and dahlia bulbs. Over the years the botanical staff has continued his legacy through research activities including plant collecting expeditions, exchanges of seed and plants with other botanical gardens all over the world, plant propagation and hybridizing, test planting, and development of a research herbarium.

13

Spring flowers, including pansies and ranunculi,
in the Shakespeare garden.

Rose Garden

The first rose garden was planted at the Huntington in 1908 as a display garden with several plants of each variety massed for color. In the 1970s the idea for a rose history walk was conceived, and now visitors can trace the story of the rose for more than a thousand years among the two thousand cultivars on display.

The oldest roses, those which date back to medieval and Renaissance times, are represented by specimens in the Shakespeare garden. The beds north of the rose arbor, with a paved walk through them, feature tea and China roses and their descendants, first introduced into Europe from China in about 1800. On the south side of the rose arbor are nineteenth-century shrub roses, descended from old European varieties. Climbing and rambling roses, from all periods and groups, grow on the arbors, arches, and pergolas.

'Picasso' roses.

The hybrid musk 'Lavender Lassie,' one of the climbing roses that grow on the pergola bordering the rose garden.

The central portion of the rose garden contains hybrid teas, floribundas, polyanthas, and miniatures. Separate beds are planted with classic pre-1920 hybrid teas and with roses from the 1920s, 1930s, and 1940s. Other beds feature roses introduced since 1950, including winners of the All-American Rose Selections and recent introductions from abroad, most notably David Austin's "Old English Roses," introduced in 1989.

David Austin's roses, the first significant new group of hybrids created since the floribundas were introduced fifty years ago, combine fragrance, growth habit, and flower form with the color range of "Old Garden Roses" (developed before 1870) and the repeat blooming characteristic of modern hybrids. These English roses exhibit the best qualities of the old rose, with the advantage that they bloom throughout the year.

Love, the Captive of Youth, encircled by 'French Lace' roses.

Shakespeare and Herb Gardens

The Shakespeare garden at the Huntington is unlike most other examples, which are usually formal knot gardens. Designed in 1983 as a setting for the new Virginia Steele Scott Gallery of American Art, this informal garden is a version of an English landscape and contains some of the plants and flowers which were cultivated in English gardens during Shakespeare's time. The site was graded to create a dell, and soil imported to raise the levels of other parts of this garden.

Its colorful, year-round blooming makes this a popular area for photography. The plays of Shakespeare mention some of the plants in this garden, including poppies, pansies, violets, pinks, carnations, rosemary, daffodils, irises, roses, columbines, and marigolds. Examples of the oldest cultivated roses are found here. Of particular historical interest are the White Rose of York and the Red Rose of Lancaster, which originated before the Christian era and were emblems of opposing factions during the fifteenth-century Wars of the Roses.

Iceland poppies in the Shakespeare garden.

The attractive formal herb garden is arranged according to the uses made of the herbs: for medicines; teas; wines and liqueurs; cooking, salads, and confections; cosmetics, perfumes, and soaps; potpourris and sachets; insect repellents; and dyes.

A variety of succulents in the desert garden: mammillaria in the foreground and behind them golden barrel cacti. Towering above is a *Chorisia* tree, with cottony masses bursting from its pods.

Desert Garden

For many visitors the most unusual part of a tour of the Botanical Gardens is the twelve-acre desert garden. More than 4,000 species of desert plants present a startling display of odd forms and shapes. The area is not intended to represent a desert — it is a landscaped garden with specimens planted where they will grow best. Many beds reflect floristic relationships, with plants grouped by geographic area.

The collection is made up of many species of xerophytes, plants that are adapted to arid environments. Though they come from various parts of the world, many xerophytes appear similar, having evolved similar strategies for survival. Some store water in their stems or leaves in order to survive in dry climates. Many protect themselves from herbivores with sharp spines or thorns, and some have waxy or woolly coverings that reflect the sun and decrease evaporation. These adaptations sometimes result in strange or even grotesquely shaped plants: the

The variegated *Agave americana*.

The brilliant orange spikes of *Aloe arborescens* dominate the desert garden in February.

ribbed and spiny barrel cactus; the columnar organ-pipe cactus; the mammillarias, cushionlike plants ranging in diameter from a few inches to three feet; and the opuntias, like the flat-jointed prickly pear or those with cylindrical joints known as cholla.

The largest cactus on the grounds is *Cereus xanthocarpus*, weighing some fifteen tons. *Cereus huntingtonianus*, with crimson buds and outside petals, was named for the founder of the institution.

Here and there are many kinds of echeverias, succulents from Mexico which vary from tiny rosettes to large, cabbage-leaved specimens more than a foot tall.

The Desert Garden Conservatory.

20

Two unusual plants in the
desert garden collection:
Welwitschia (above) and
Lithops (right).

This colorful *Epiphyllum* blooms during the day.
The Huntington also has a large collection
of white night-flowering cacti.

At the upper end of the garden is a conservatory housing vulnerable succulents. Some of the plants demonstrate mimicry (those that imitate stones); others produce windows (transparent leaf-tips that transmit sunlight); and still others exhibit convergence (plants that look similar but are only distantly related).

Among the notable collections are species of *Lithops*, South African members of the ice plant family famed for their resemblance to stones. In nature, each species grows on ground of the same color. Red-leaved *Lithops aucampiae* grows almost completely buried in reddish soil, the whitish *Lithops gracilidelineata* among white quartz pebbles. Tiny *Titanopsis calcarea*, of the same family, looks so much like the surface of the limestone rocks on which it grows that it was discovered accidentally by an African botanist who leaned against a rock and crushed a plant with his hand.

Cacti that are quite atypical are the epiphytic (tree-dwelling) species native to the moist forest areas of Latin America. They are relatively spineless, with flattened leaflike stems best displayed in a hanging basket. The Huntington has one of the world's largest collections. One plant that is of the utmost importance botanically is *Welwitschia mirabilis*. It is bizarre in appearance — the species name means "marvelous," an adjective well deserved. Scattered along the rainless desert of coastal Namibia and Angola, the leaves of these ancient plants lie sprawled like so many stranded sea monsters. During its long lifetime *Welwitschia* has only its original two leaves, which become frayed and torn by desert winds as they grow to a length of ten feet. The most striking fact about *Welwitschia* is that it is not a flowering plant at all — it bears cones and is a distant relative of the conifers and cycads. Like the gingko, *Welwitschia* has been called a "living fossil."

Creeping devil cacti in the Baja California bed of the desert garden.

The Japanese house, surrounded by informal plantings of camellias, azaleas, wisteria, and flowering fruit trees, overlooks the moon bridge and pond.

Japanese Garden

West of the rose garden is the Japanese garden, distinguished by curving walks, flowing water, and small, still lakes; artistically placed stones and statuary; and painstakingly pruned and trained plants. There are no broad vistas or symmetrical plantings, common in many European gardens. The garden is planned to inspire a tranquil and contemplative state of mind for the visitor who is not in a hurry.

The entrance gateway, guarded by two half-dog, half-lion figures, has special significance for the Japanese. Any person entering a gateway is expected to assume a quiet, alert mental attitude that will bring him or her into harmony with the place being visited.

When Mr. Huntington acquired the ranch, the present Japanese garden was a rugged gorge surrounded by a tangle of trees, wild grapevines, and poison oak. In 1911 major construction was undertaken to build terraces, ponds, and paths, and install a Japanese tea garden purchased intact from its Pasadena owner. The purchase included twenty-five truckloads of mature plants and a complete house that had to be sawed apart, transported, and reassembled.

Parts of this five-room house came originally from Japan. One room is arranged for the tea ceremony. In an alcove, or tokonoma, a "tea-flower" arrangement consisting of one or two flowers with leaves and graceful grasses or branches gives a feeling of relaxation and freshness. The tokonoma in the other room contains a traditional Japanese flower arrangement, or ikebana, created in the style of the Ikenobo school, the oldest school of Japanese flower arranging. Members of the San Marino League provide the flower arrangements and furnishings in the house.

The moon bridge in the Japanese garden.

Among the other notable structures in the garden are the temple bell and the moon bridge. The bell is of Buddhist origin and its inscription states that it was cast in 1766 for Kongo Buji Temple on Mt. Koya, an important religious sanctuary in Japan.

Moon bridges were a feature of Chinese garden architecture, adopted by the Japanese in the thirteenth century. The large, rounded bridge is usually known as a moon bridge because the arch and the reflection in the water below form a full moon shape, and also because "moon viewing" from beneath the bridge was a diversion for estate owners cruising on their private lakes. Dominating the scene around the bridge is a weeping willow, a native of China. Near the other end are unusually large specimens of *Cycas revoluta* (cycads).

The garden features many other plants commonly found in a Japanese garden, including the Japanese maple, Japanese red and black pines, azaleas, and camellias. In front of the Japanese house is an extensive planting of azaleas, which flower from February to April. Paths lead north from the house through part of the camellia collection. Beneath a canopy of live oak and pine trees, the sides of the canyon are covered with many cultivars of camellias.

In 1968 the Japanese garden was expanded with the addition of a Zen garden, reached by a zigzag bridge. It overlooks a "dry streambed" where rocks and pebbles simulate water. Two towering Canary Island pines stand at the far end of the bridge.

Above the zigzag bridge, a tile-capped, earth-colored wall surrounds the dry Zen garden. This type of garden was introduced into Japan from China along with

23

The zigzag bridge, which spans the canyon between the Japanese house and the Zen garden.

Zen Buddhism. Within the walls is a slate walk passing through the center of the garden. To the east, ginkgo trees, which come from China and are related to the conifers, and mondo grass ground cover form a small garden designed to represent a forest. To the west is the dry garden, an open expanse of raked gravel in a pattern suggestive of flowing water. It is broken here and there by rocks and backed by a curve of trees and shrubs suggesting a far bank. This garden is inspired by the main garden at Daito-kuji, near Kyoto, created in the mid-sixteenth century.

The Zen garden.

In the courtyard beyond the Zen garden is a representative collection of bonsai, or Japanese dwarfed trees. Bonsai culture is a Japanese art form now comparatively well known in the West. The aim is to produce trees in miniature, whether a whole grove or a single gnarled, weather-twisted patriarch. Examples of suiseki, an art form which has only recently been introduced to the American public, are also displayed here. A suiseki is a water-sculpted stone, carefully chosen to represent a natural phenomenon such as a distant mountain, a cascade, or an island in the sea.

Flowering peach next to a stone pagoda in the canyon of the Japanese garden.

24

Wisteria in flower.

Cycads

The cycad collection at the Huntington is one of the oldest in the United States. Examples can be seen in the jungle garden, the Australian garden, the courtyard and circle northeast of the Art Gallery, and the Japanese, desert, and palm gardens.

The collection was started in 1910 with a few plants collected in Mexico. In 1913 some exceptional specimens arrived from Japan, including plants said to be between 300 and 400 years old. Among these may have been the large clumps of *Cycas revoluta* near the Art Gallery and in the Japanese garden.

These "living fossils" are relics of an ancient and extensive cycad flora that thrived alongside the dinosaurs in the early Mesozoic era. Today most cycads are found in dry, open country and are restricted to warmer regions of the world, such as Australia, southeast Asia, southern Africa, and Mexico.

Palmlike in appearance, cycads are in fact more closely related to pines, and they produce cones with toxic seed. Cycads grow extremely slowly and most species do not exceed ten feet in height.

The cycads at the Huntington are among the oldest plants on the grounds.

Subtropical and Jungle Gardens

To visitors from the colder parts of the United States, many of the plants at the Huntington seem tropical. But many of the woody garden plants grown in Southern California are actually subtropical, an arbitrary but convenient term for plants from regions that have occasional frosts but not severe freezes. Although there are such plants in the desert, palm, and Australian gardens, the subtropical garden features them extensively. Subtropical plants thrive in the Mediterranean climate characteristic of California, with its warm, dry summers and mild winters, during which most of the rain falls. This garden also includes plants from western Australia, the Cape Provinces of South Africa, parts of Chile, and the Mediterranean itself.

The four-acre garden covers the slope below the Art Gallery and extends from the Japanese garden to the jungle garden. Until the twentieth century, it was covered with oaks and grasses, and coast live oaks are still to be seen here. One of the paths was part of the road that was used by the Huntingtons and their neighbors, the Pattons, when they visited one another.

Prominent in the garden are various species of *Tabebuia*, spectacular flowering trees, and a forest of jacarandas, a Brazilian tree with a dazzling show of blue flowers in late spring. Yellow-flowering cassias are well

Australian Garden

With a landmass roughly the size of the United States, Australia is home to over 25,000 species of plants, most of them found nowhere else. The five-acre Australian garden was created to display trees and shrubs from this flora which are suitable for local use. Its finest display is in early spring, beginning with the blooming of the acacias and continuing on through the flowering of the kangaroo paws, melaleucas, wax flowers, and blue hibiscus.

Some of the smaller, shrublike eucalypts are extremely pretty, with red, pink, or bright yellow flowers, while varieties of the well-known bottlebrush become flaming masses of scarlet. Among the most profusely flowering is the mint bush (*Prostanthera*), with aromatic leaves and masses of purple blossoms.

Among the unusual plants in this garden are the kangaroo paws, named for the shape of their intriguing red, green, or yellow flowers. The most startling is the red and green kangaroo paw (*Anigozanthus manglesii*), with its brilliant red flower stalks and pure emerald-green flowers.

The waterfall in the subtropical garden, with flowering bromeliads.

Lily pond in the jungle garden with giant bird of paradise, calla lilies, bamboo, and *Cordyline australis*.

represented, both as shrubs and large trees. Along one path is *Bauhinia blakeana,* the most resplendent of the orchid trees, with deep mauve flowers. Only one plant of this tree was ever discovered in

Cymbidiums growing outdoors in the jungle garden.

the wild, in the hills above Hong Kong, and all existing cultivated trees are its descendants.

The jungle garden contains plants chosen to recreate the atmosphere of a tropical forest, including gingers, ferns, palms, bamboo, and many members of the calla lily family. Orchids, certain ferns, and bromeliads grow above the paths on the limbs and trunks of trees just as they do in tropical forests.

Palm Garden

Most palms grow in the wet, tropical regions of the world, but about 300 species will survive the low rainfall and cool winters of Southern California. Most of these are represented in the palm garden and adjacent jungle garden. Palms were a particular interest of Mr. Huntington's, especially because of their suitability for the Southern California landscape.

27

Lotus flower in the lower lily ponds.

Camellia japonica
'Grandiflora rosea variegated,'
one of the species of camellia
bordering the North Vista.

North Vista and Camellia Collection

The North Vista's combination of greenery, flowering shrubs, and long lines of sculpture is reminiscent of a seventeenth-century European garden. The stone statues surrounding the lawn portray allegorical and mythologi-cal subjects; most were made in the seventeenth century. The large stone fountain at the far end of the North Vista comes from Italy and is a handsome example of the early baroque style in sculpture.

The garden surrounding the North Vista contains cultivars of the three principal species of camellias (*Camellia sasanqua, Camellia japonica,* and *Camellia reticulata*) and numerous azaleas that bloom from December to early spring. Other species of camellias are represented in the Huntington collection, either here or in the North Canyon, next to the Japanese garden. One of these is *Camellia sinensis,* whose leaves are harvested for tea.

Art Gallery Garden

The area is dominated by the giant bird of paradise (*Strelitzia nicolai*) from South Africa, with specimens of the more common bird of paradise (*Strelitzia reginae*) nearby. One of the more unusual trees in this garden is the white floss silk tree (*Chorisia insignis*) from Peru. In the autumn and winter its bare branches are covered with white flowers; in the spring it bears large seed pods which burst open with a shower of whitish, kapok-like fibers. Also here is a collection of mature cycads; some large specimens are about 500 years old. On the walls of the gallery's covered passageway are two species of staghorn ferns (*Platycerium*) from Australia and Indonesia. In the wild, these ferns cling to tree branches or to cliffs.

Courtyard garden at the entrance to the Huntington Gallery, with fountain and bronze statue *Bacchante* by American sculptor Frederick MacMonnies (1863-1937).

Eighteenth-century French terra-cotta statue *Diana*, signed "Fremin 1717," on the loggia of the Art Gallery.
The original stone figure by René Frémin (1672-1744) is now in the Louvre.

Garden Sculpture

One of the most delightful and distinctive features of the Huntington gardens is the sculpture. Most of it dates from the late seventeenth and early eighteenth centuries and was made in northern Italy, southern Germany, and France.

Most garden sculpture, including that at the Huntington, was intended to be part of a larger ensemble. The themes are often vague and the execution sketchy, but the pieces are frequently charming and entertaining. Amatory episodes usually have a prominent place. Near the entrance to the Shakespeare Garden, for instance, Love is blindfolding Youth; in the Rose Garden, Love is the captive of Youth; and no less a person than Louis XV is shown guided by Love in the Neo-Palladian tempietto on the south lawn below the Art Gallery.

The long rows of single figures lining either side of the North Vista were made before 1750 and came from the grounds of a villa near Padua. Some figures are easy to identify, such as Perseus with the head of Medusa, or Athena in her helmet and armor; but others are more difficult to place. Two very lumpy and muscle-bound figures of Time and Truth are certainly of independent origin, probably south German.

Probably the most charming of the garden figures are the four large terra-cottas on the loggia of the Art Gallery. Each is signed by a prominent French sculptor of the seventeenth or eighteenth century. While these sculptors executed the marbles on which these terra-cottas are based, it is unlikely that they were personally responsible for the Huntington figures.

Marble statue *Cupid Blindfolding Youth* (detail),
in the seventeenth-century Italian temple
at the entrance to the North Vista.

The Art Collections

he Huntington Art Collections are specialized in character, focusing on eighteenth-century British and French art, and on American art ranging from the early eighteenth century to the early twentieth. Perhaps the best-known part of the collections is a group of British portraits from the late eighteenth century. Other objects of the same period round out the collection: French paintings, French and British sculpture, tapestries, furniture, porcelain, and silver, and British drawings and watercolors. The large quantity of distinguished furniture and decorative objects provides a congenial setting for the paintings and creates a vivid picture of the accoutrements with which the aristocratic and wealthy members of late eighteenth-century society surrounded themselves.

The American art displayed in the Virginia Steele Scott Gallery consists of paintings, sculpture, and the decorative arts. The Dorothy Collins Brown wing features a full spectrum of the furniture designed by turn-of-the-century Pasadena architects Charles and Henry Greene. The Huntington also has important collections of American drawings, prints, and photographs.

The collections are not static. The core of the British collection, including many of the most famous paintings, was assembled by Henry E. Huntington between 1910 and his death in 1927. But the collections have continued to grow by both gift and purchase, particularly in the areas of American art, drawings and watercolors, sculpture, silver, and furniture.

The main hall of the Art Gallery, with the bronze statue
Diana Huntress, 1782, by Jean-Antoine Houdon.

Thomas Gainsborough (1727-88), *Karl Friedrich Abel*, c. 1777, oil on canvas.

inclination as a collector was to specialize — whether it was in early English books, desert plants, or British portraits — to build a great collection around a limited area rather than spread his attention thinly over a wide range of interests.

Many of the finest works by the most gifted English artists of the period were large formal portraits. Although most of the pictures were commissioned by the sitter, many were also intended for public display. They made their initial appearances at the annual Royal Academy exhibition, which was then the principal artistic event of the year. A somewhat grand and rhetorical air was considered appropriate for this type of painting, and this artistic intention should be kept in mind when looking at the portraits in the Huntington collection.

Most of the people represented in these portraits knew each other. They belonged to a small, close-knit, and privileged segment of British society. Some led active and interesting lives with the result that we know a good deal about them. Others, although equally well placed, left almost no record of themselves.

British Art

The British collection is remarkable for its coherence, its specialized character, and its dedication to the art of a particular time and place. In this respect it is different from the other great American art collections that were developed at the same time: those of Henry Clay Frick, P. A. B. Widener, Andrew W. Mellon, and Isabella Stewart Gardner, to name the most prominent. The Huntington offers opportunities for the study of British art of the eighteenth and early nineteenth century in a collection that for quality, variety, and depth cannot be surpassed outside London.

Visitors often wonder why the Huntingtons chose to concentrate their collecting as they did. The answer lies partly in Mr. Huntington's book and manuscript collections, which were focused on Anglo-American civilization and growing rapidly at the time the art collection was being formed. In addition, Mr. Huntington's personal

British Paintings

The Huntington Gallery houses a group of twenty full-length portraits created between 1770 and 1800 by Joshua Reynolds, Thomas Gainsborough, George Romney, and Thomas Lawrence, including such famous pictures as *The Blue Boy, Pinkie,* and *Mrs. Siddons as the Tragic Muse.*

Thomas Gainsborough (1727-88), *Juliana, Lady Petre,* 1788, oil on canvas.

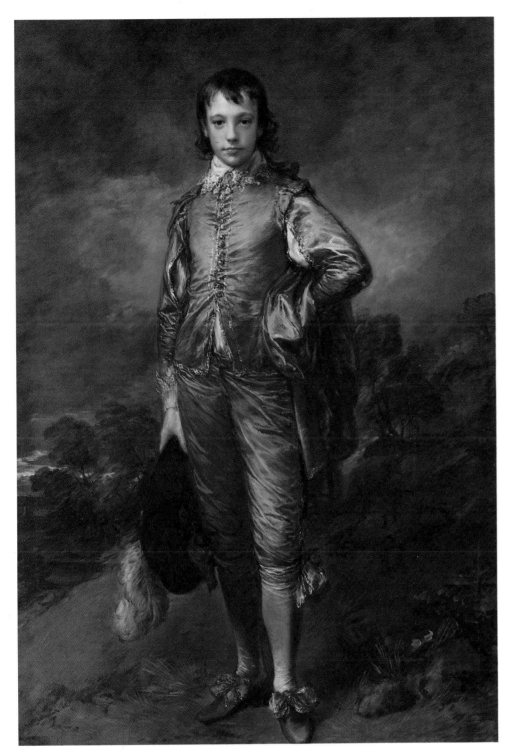

33

The most famous portraits are displayed in the Main Gallery, which was added to the residence in 1934 to display the larger pictures to better advantage.

The most celebrated painting in this room, Gainsborough's *The Blue Boy* (c. 1770), represents Jonathan Buttall, the son of a successful hardware merchant who was a close friend of the artist's. Gainsborough dressed the boy in a costume familiar through the portraits of the great Flemish artist, Anthony Van Dyck, who lived and

worked in England during the early seventeenth century. Gainsborough had unbounded admiration for the work of Van Dyck and seems to have planned *The Blue Boy* as an act of homage to him.

Seven other of Gainsborough's finest works hang in the Main Gallery (in all, twelve of his paintings are on display throughout the building). It is interesting to compare the paint application in *The Blue Boy*, the earliest of these, with that in the portrait *Juliana, Lady Petre* (1788),

34

nearly twenty years later. As Gainsborough matured he became more assured, able to make a few brushstrokes suggest a tree, a skirt, or even a whole figure. For sheer virtuosity in the manipulation of paint on canvas he can be considered one of the greatest artists that England has produced.

Thomas Lawrence's *Pinkie* (1794) faces *The Blue Boy* and is often paired with it in popular esteem, but it was painted about twenty-five years later than Gainsborough's masterpiece

George Romney (1734-1802), *Lady Hamilton in a Straw Hat,* before 1785, oil on canvas.

and had no association with the earlier painting until they both arrived at the Huntington in the 1920s. The young girl, Sarah Barrett Moulton, was born in Jamaica to a wealthy plantation family. The portrait was painted on commission for her grandmother after the girl came to England for her education. Unfortunately Sarah died within a few months of the time the portrait was completed. Her brother, who later owned the painting, was the father of the poet Elizabeth Barrett Browning.

Joshua Reynolds (1723-92), *Sarah Siddons as the Tragic Muse*, 1784, oil on canvas.

Another portrait in the room, Joshua Reynolds's *Sarah Siddons as the Tragic Muse* (1784), is generally regarded as one of that artist's greatest works. It represents the then leading actress of the English stage, who specialized in tragic roles. The painting is a complex composition, filled with visual references to Michelangelo, Rembrandt, Aristotle, Ripa's *Iconologia*, and theories of the passions, all of which were understood well enough by Reynolds's contemporaries but are not likely to be familiar to present-

Joshua Reynolds (1723-92), *Jane, Countess of Harrington*, 1777-79, oil on canvas.

George Romney (1734-1802), *The Beckford Children*, 1789-91, oil on canvas.

J. M. W. Turner (1775-1851),
The Grand Canal, Venice: Shylock,
c. 1837, oil on canvas.

day spectators. Yet even without these additional levels of meaning, the painting stands in purely visual terms as one of the grandest and most dignified of British portraits.

While portraits were the leading art form in late eighteenth-century Britain, landscape became the more popular subject for paintings in the early nineteenth century. The period was dominated by two giants, John Constable and J. M. W. Turner, who overshadowed a host of other highly gifted artists. These men were contemporary rivals, and two of the greatest artists that England ever produced.

Turner was fascinated by light and color. Partly for this reason he was drawn to the brilliant skies, marble palaces, and shimmering lagoons of Venice. His *Grand Canal, Venice* (c. 1837) is a work from the latter part of his career. He is also represented in the collection by *Neapolitan Fisher Girls Surprised Bathing by Moonlight* (1840). This painting reveals his concern with abstract areas of light and color rather than details of things represented.

Constable's *View on the Stour near Dedham* (1822), in the Main Gallery, is considered one of the outstanding achievements not only of British but also of European landscape painting. The painting depicts a quiet stretch of country in eastern England within a couple of miles of Constable's birthplace. He painted various views of this area throughout his life, and seems never to have tired of studying the different moods created by changes in

weather and atmosphere.

If Mr. and Mrs. Huntington were to walk through the Art Gallery today, they would see much that is familiar. But they would also see many items new to them: the British sculpture, the silver, the sporting and genre paintings, the conversation-piece portraits, and a fair amount of British furniture.

John Constable (1776-1837),
View on the Stour near Dedham,
1822, oil on canvas.

British Sculpture, Furniture, Silver, and Ceramics

A fine representative collection of British sculpture, assembled since the 1960s, is on display throughout the Huntington Gallery. The most important piece historically, and one of the most attractive visually, is an approximately half-scale model executed in 1796 by Joseph Wilton for a commemorative monument to Archbishop Tillotson.

By and large the British furniture acquired by the Huntingtons was for day-to-day use rather than for show. While much of it is of good and even excellent quality, comparatively few pieces reach the level of artistic interest of the British paintings or of the French decorative arts in the collections. A number of pieces of British furniture were added in 1938 when Mrs. Charles H. Quinn of

The Quinn Room. The paneling and most of the furniture in this room, from three different eighteenth-century British houses, were donated by Florence M. Quinn of Los Angeles.

Los Angeles presented her collection to the Huntington. Most of her collection, which included paintings and Chinese porcelain as well as furniture, is now installed on the second floor, in a paneled room typical of the drawing room of a well-to-do English family in the middle of the eighteenth century.

The silver collection, now numbering about 400 pieces, ranges in date from the fifteenth to the mid-nineteenth century and covers a wider span chronologically than any other facet of British art on display in the gallery. Selections from the silver collection are distributed over both floors, with the most important concentrations in the North Passage and the Dining Room. Upstairs is one of the most famous pieces, John Flaxman's silver-gilt *Shield of Achilles* (1821), which is an outstanding example of English neoclassic art.

Most of the ceramics in the Huntington Gallery are part of an important collection of mid-eighteenth-century pieces from the Chelsea porcelain factory, famous for ornamental pieces like vases, potpourri jars, and small figures. The Chelsea porcelain is displayed in the Main and West halls on the ground floor of the gallery.

Silver-gilt Rosewater Ewer and Basin, made in London in 1607.

37

Anthony Van Dyck (1559-1642),
Anne Killigrew, Mrs. Kirke,
c. 1638, oil on canvas.

European Painting

The representation of eighteenth-century French and other European painting was greatly strengthened in 1978 when Judge and Mrs. Lucius P. Green bequeathed the Adele S. Browning Memorial Collection to the Huntington. The paintings and other works of art in the bequest are shown as a unit in adjoining rooms on the second floor of the Huntington Gallery. Many of the leading French painters of the "ancien régime" are represented here: Watteau, Pater, Lancret, Nattier, Boucher, Fragonard, Hubert Robert, Drouais, Greuze, and Prudhon. The portraits, landscapes, genre subjects, and distinctive *fêtes galantes,* in which elegant men and women disport themselves in rural surroundings, are typical of rococo art.

Dutch and Flemish seventeenth-century paintings are also represented, including the well-known *Lady with a Plume* (1636), which was produced in Rembrandt's studio. Like Rembrandt portraits of this period, it demonstrates the care taken with details of face and costume.

Jean-Baptiste Greuze (1725-1805), *Young Knitter Asleep,* oil on canvas.

European Influences on British Art

The Flemish artist Anthony Van Dyck (1559-1641) had a strong influence on English portraiture during the last half of the eighteenth century. Van Dyck had worked for Charles I in the 1630s, and his most notable work in the Huntington collection, *Anne Killigrew, Mrs. Kirke,* is of a lady of the court. The painting hangs at the top of the grand staircase in the Huntington Gallery.

The Italian painter Canaletto (1697-1768) is also represented here, with two sparkling views of Venice. Canaletto's presence in a gallery dominated by British eighteenth-century painting is particularly appropriate. Not only were his works avidly collected by Englishmen as souvenirs of their "grand tours," but Canaletto, who came to England, had a direct influence on the development of English landscape painting.

38

The Library Room features late seventeenth-century Savonnerie carpets, mid-eighteenth-century Beauvais wall tapestries, Gobelins chair tapestries, and library tables (detail below).

French Decorative Art

The Huntington's collection of French furniture and decorative art, dating mostly from the eighteenth century, is one of the finest in America. Probably at no time in history has more skill and artistry gone into the design and construction of fine furniture than in France during the half century before the Revolution. All crafts concerned with the decorative arts, and especially furniture making, tapestry weaving, and porcelain manufacture, were extensively patronized by the court and aristocracy. Time and money were no object and the quality of the fin-

ished product was always of the highest order.

Furniture (from small writing tables to chairs and large chests), tapestries, Sèvres porcelain, and decorative objects (primarily clocks and candelabra) are all represented in the collection by examples of great artistic importance. They illustrate the various styles that dominated French art from the late seventeenth until the late eighteenth century. Displays of these items can be found throughout the Huntington Gallery and the Arabella D. Huntington Memorial Collection.

Jean-Antoine Houdon (1741-1828), *Portrait of a Lady* (so-called Baroness de la Houze), 1777, marble.

Of particular interest is the large paneled library room on the ground floor of the Huntington Gallery, which gives the impression of a grand French salon in the mid-eighteenth century. The sumptuous and elegant furnishings would have been found in a royal palace or the chateau of a wealthy aristocrat. The earliest objects are two carpets made in the late seventeenth century at the Savonnerie factory for Louis XIV, originally part of the furnishings of the Louvre. The four splendid wall tapestries (a fifth in the suite is located in the hall outside the library) were designed by François Boucher (1703-70). They were woven at the Beauvais factory in the mid-eighteenth century and, like the carpets, appear to have been a royal commission. The tapestries covering the chairs and settees (again from the mid-eighteenth century, but woven at the Gobelins factory) almost certainly belonged to the mistress of Louis XV, Mme. de Pompadour.

French decorative art was always a special interest of Mrs. Huntington's. As a grand, final expression of affection to his wife, Mr. Huntington purchased some exquisite works in 1927 to form the basis of the Arabella D. Huntington Memorial Collection, which is housed in the Library building.

One room in the Memorial is devoted to French porcelain and features lavishly decorated ornamental pieces of Sèvres porcelain from the eighteenth century. Adjacent is a room of French furniture, where one can survey the evolution of French design from the middle to the end of the eighteenth century. On the walls are tapestries designed by François Boucher, part of his "Italian Village Scenes," woven on the Beauvais looms. Around the room are clocks, torchères, candelabras, commodes, and tables.

Hubert Robert (1733-1808), *Women Washing at a Fountain*, oil on canvas.

French Sculpture

The French sculpture at the Huntington comprises one of the finest collections of its kind in this country. It consists of marbles, bronzes, and terra-cottas, mostly from the second half of the eighteenth century. The sculpture, like the French furniture, reflects the aristocratic elegance generally associated with that epoch. Most of the French sculpture is displayed in the Arabella D. Huntington Memorial Collection.

The principal sculptor represented is Jean-Antoine Houdon, one of the great artists of the eighteenth century. His *Portrait of a Lady* (1777) is one of the most important pieces in the collection. There are also objects made by (or designed by) J. B. Pigalle, Falconet, and Clodion.

Renaissance Bronzes

The collection of Renaissance bronzes displayed in the small library in the Huntington Gallery is of particularly high quality. Most of the bronzes were produced in Italy, or in other parts of Europe by sculptors who had close contact with Italian art. The collection is especially rich in the work of the sixteenth-century sculptor Giovanni Bologna and his followers. The majority of the bronzes were purchased by Mr. Huntington en bloc from the great collection of Renaissance bronzes formed by J. Pierpont Morgan.

Although small in size (mostly between ten and twenty inches high), they exhibit the same strong sense of design and pattern found in larger sculptures. In *Nessus and Deïanira*, for example, the twist of the body of Deïanira echoes the twist of the body of the centaur, and the limbs and drapery add to the movement of the whole piece.

Renaissance bronzes display elegance, virtuosity, and meticulous craftsmanship. They are objects for the connoisseur, intended for close study.

41

Renaissance Paintings

A small group of Renaissance paintings is on display in the Arabella D. Huntington Memorial Collection. The paintings were collected by Arabella Huntington for her New York residence and bequeathed to her son Archer, from whom they were acquired by Mr. Huntington for the Memorial Collection. The most important painting in the group is the *Madonna and Child* by the Flemish fifteenth-century artist Roger van der Weyden — a major artist whose few identified works are considered masterpieces of Flemish Renaissance painting.

Giovanni Bologna (1529-1608),
Nessus and Deïanira,
late sixteenth century, bronze.

British Drawings and Watercolors

With approximately 17,000 British drawings and watercolors, the Huntington has one of the most impressive collections outside London. While Mr. Huntington acquired a few notable groups of drawings by Blake, Rowlandson, Cosway, and the Cruikshanks, the majority of the collection has been assembled since the 1950s, when a serious program was launched to acquire British drawings as a complement to the paintings in the Huntington Gallery.

More than 500 artists are represented in the collection, covering all the important phases of British draftsmanship for the period 1600 to 1900. The collection includes large holdings of artists such as Thomas Rowlandson, among the most popular and immediately appealing of British artists, who is represented by over 500 items.

Many of the drawings Mr. Huntington acquired appeared in extra-illustrated books. Extra-illustrating books was a popular practice in the eighteenth and nineteenth centuries. A volume would be taken out of its binding, prints and drawings mounted and inserted between the pages, and the whole bound back together again. A book could be expanded by several volumes in the process.

Edward Norgate (c. 1581-1650), *Judith Norgate*, c. 1613, watercolor on ivory.

British Miniature Portraits

The painting of miniature portraits flourished in England from the late sixteenth to the early nineteenth centuries and often commanded the talents of artists of great distinction. The Huntington collection is particularly strong in examples from the later part of this period, which echo the grand-manner mode of presentation seen in the full-length British portraits. There is also a fine group of miniatures by masters from the seventeenth century.

Miniatures were usually given as tokens of love or affection, much as we give photographs today. They were frequently worn as jewelry by both men and women and often framed in precious stones. Normally they were painted in opaque watercolor on vellum or ivory and encased in glass. Frequently the back of the locket contained a decorative design made from the hair of the person represented.

Richard Cosway (1742-1821), *George, Prince of Wales*, 1787, watercolor on ivory.

Thomas Rowlandson (1756-1827),
A French Frigate Towing an English Man-o'-War into Port,
c. 1790, pen and watercolor over pencil.

William Blake (1757-1827),
The Conversion of Saul,
c. 1800, pen and watercolor.

43

William Blake . . . Remarkable Poet, Distinctive Painter

The Huntington has the most comprehensive collection in America of original watercolors, pencil drawings, manuscripts, engravings, and books by William Blake. The diversity of the collection makes it invaluable to scholars, who come from around the world to study this English poet and artist of the late eighteenth and early nineteenth centuries. His work as a painter, poet, and printmaker challenges the usual practice of separating these arts into different disciplines. Understanding one facet of Blake's work requires attention to all the others.

The richness of the Huntington's Blake holdings is best exemplified by a splendid collection of the hand-colored books of his poetry. Illuminated books, a composite art in which poetry and painting are inextricably intertwined, are considered Blake's finest and most char-

acteristic achievements. In all, he wrote, etched, and decorated some sixteen books of his own poetry, of which the Huntington has eleven. Blake prepared few copies of each work, since they were all done by hand and the demand was small. The average number of copies of each book seems to have been about a dozen.

Blake had limited recognition as a poet and painter during his lifetime. Today, however, he is held in the highest esteem by critics, scholars, collectors, and connoisseurs. His works are among the most popular subjects in our exhibitions. There is often a display of Blake material in the Library Exhibition Hall, where individual items are shown for limited periods of time. His watercolors and other designs are included in occasional temporary exhibitions in the Huntington Art Gallery.

The Virginia Steele Scott Gallery of American Art, viewed here across the Shakespeare garden, draws its design from other classically inspired buildings on the grounds.

American Art

The Virginia Steele Scott Gallery, opened in 1984, and the collection it houses were a gift from the Scott Foundation in memory of Mrs. Scott, who was an art collector, patron, and philanthropist. Prior to 1984, the Huntington art collections had been identified primarily with British art of the eighteenth and early nineteenth centuries. However, it had been the hope of Mr. Huntington and his advisers that the art collections might be expanded into the American field in later years when the opportunity arose.

The Gallery currently exhibits paintings, sculpture, and decorative arts from the eighteenth to the early twentieth century. The collection was augmented in 1990 with a display featuring the work of Pasadena architects Charles and Henry Greene. The gallery also houses collections of American drawings, prints, and photographs, which form the basis for special exhibitions each year.

George Caleb Bingham (1811-1879),
In a Quandary, 1851, oil on canvas

John Singleton Copley
(1738-1815), *Sarah Jackson*,
c. 1765, oil on canvas.

Though the chronological boundaries of the American art collection are open, the pictures it now contains were painted between the 1740s and the 1930s. The earliest include portraits by John Smibert, Robert Feke, and John Singleton Copley; the latest include works by John Stuart Curry, Walt Kuhn, and Edward Hopper. The collection illustrates the range of American painting for the period covered, demonstrating the shift from portraiture in the eighteenth century to landscape, still-life, and genre painting in the nineteenth. Many of the works also show where American artists sought stylistic inspiration: frequently in England in the eighteenth and early nineteenth centuries, and increasingly in France in the late

nineteenth and early twentieth centuries. In addition, the collection reveals the interest shown by American nineteenth- and early twentieth-century artists in cultural and economic changes that transformed America from an agrarian to an industrial society and that continuously pushed west the American frontier.

The principal space for the display of the paintings is a large skylit gallery in the form of a Greek cross. Each of the four arms of the cross displays a group of thematically connected paintings. The first is devoted primarily to American portraits of the eighteenth and early nineteenth centuries. The other three feature narrative and genre subjects, landscapes, and early twentieth-century art.

Mary Cassatt (1845-1926), *Breakfast in Bed*, 1897, oil on canvas.

Most of the paintings are characteristic works by the artists concerned. John Singleton Copley's portrayal of Sarah Jackson (c. 1765) is a sophisticated example of the colonial artist's grand-manner style. Ammi Phillips's depiction of Hannah Bull Thompson (1824) effectively displays the itinerant artist's naive but bold approach to portraiture. George Caleb Bingham's *In a Quandary* (1851) is a powerful examination of the Mississippi riverboat men who connected eastern civilization with the western frontier. Frederic Edwin Church's *Chimborazo* (1864) is a monumental, romantic rendering of the South American landscape by a renowned member of the Hudson River School. William Merritt Chase's *Tenth Street Studio* is a self-reflective exploration of the late-nineteenth-century artist's fascination with Middle Eastern and Asian cultures. Mary

Cassatt's *Breakfast in Bed* (1897) is one of the most eloquent of the painter's many impressionistic treatments of the mother-and-child theme. Edward Hopper's *The Long Leg* (1935), with its simple, strong color scheme, indicates his response to the growing interest in abstraction in the early twentieth century.

In the four arms of the Main Gallery, examples of American furniture from the eighteenth century to the early twentieth are exhibited along with the paintings. The furnishings in the central area are from the American Craftsman period at the turn of the century. The collections are also complemented by examples of nineteenth- and early twentieth-century American sculpture, including Harriet Hosmer's *Puck* (after 1854) and Frederic Remington's *Bronco Buster* (1895).

Edward Hopper
(1882-1967),
The Long Leg,
c. 1935,
oil on canvas.

William Merritt Chase (1849-1916), *Tenth Street Studio,* c. 1880, oil on canvas.

Frederic Edwin Church (1826-1900), *Chimborazo*, 1864, oil on canvas.

Thomas Moran
(1837-1926),
*Rock Towers of the
Rio Virgin*, 1908,
oil on canvas.

Greene & Greene and the American Arts and Crafts Movement

Inlay detail from a Greene & Greene table
(William R. Thorsen house, 1909).

In the Dorothy Collins Brown wing of the Scott Gallery is a permanent exhibition of furniture and decorative arts by the American architects Charles and Henry Greene who, in the early twentieth century, produced buildings and furnishings which were renowned for their design and craftsmanship.

The main hall of the exhibition features the brothers' designs for both furniture and decorative objects. In the adjacent gallery, the dining room of the Robinson house (1906, Pasadena) has been reconstructed, reuniting furniture and chandelier for the first time in half a century. The Thorsen house sideboard in the main hall and the Robinson house dining room chandelier are among the most important remaining examples of Greene & Greene furnishings. A third major feature of the exhibition is the reassembled staircase from the Arthur A. Libby house (Pasadena, 1905; demolished in 1968).

The exhibition is a cooperative venture between the Huntington and the Gamble House, University of Southern California.

Reconstruction of the dining room of the
Henry M. Robinson house, 1906.

The Book & Manuscript Collections

r. Huntington was interested in book collecting nearly all of his life. He treasured to the end one of his boyhood books, *Songs for the Little Ones at Home,* which he kept in a specially made morocco case among the volumes of which he was fondest.

Between 1911 and 1925 Mr. Huntington acquired a number of very important libraries. In fact, he bought so many entire libraries that his collection was known as the "library of libraries." Among these was the Church Library, purchased for a reputed $1,000,000, which included the manuscript autobiography of Benjamin Franklin, twelve Shakespeare folios and thirty-seven quartos, and rare first editions of Spenser and Milton. From the famous collection of Robert Hoe, Mr. Huntington purchased a copy of the Gutenberg Bible for the then-record price of $50,000, which attracted international attention.

After 1914, Mr. Huntington turned to England to purchase other important collections — among them the Kemble-Devonshire collection of English plays; twenty-five books printed by William Caxton, England's first printer; and the Bridgewater Library, perhaps the greatest British family library dating from the sixteenth century. The Bridgewater Library's 4,400 printed books and nearly 12,000 manuscripts included the Ellesmere Chaucer, the most celebrated manuscript of the *Canterbury Tales.*

Today the Library contains more than four times as many books as it did when Mr. Huntington died in 1927. Included are more than 600,000 rare and reference books; thousands of photographs, prints, microforms, and ephemera; and over three million individual manuscripts.

The nearly 2,000 scholars (called "readers") who use the Library's research materials each year are attracted by what one scholar has called "perhaps the most wonderful research environment in the world."

The main reading room of the Huntington Library.

The Ellesmere manuscript of *The Canterbury Tales*, with what is thought to be the earliest known portrait of Chaucer (c. 1410). Below is one of the pilgrims, the Wife of Bath.

The Ellesmere Chaucer and Medieval Manuscripts

The Library has records unequaled in the United States for the study of medieval England. The collection contains several thousand English medieval documents of great historical, literary, and religious interest.

Before the development of printing in the fifteenth century, all books and documents were written by hand. The earliest important manuscript book in the Library is the Gundulf Bible, which dates from the first decades after the Norman Conquest of England in 1066. The most important medieval manuscript added since the death of Mr. Huntington is the beautiful Ambrosiaster, a Latin commentary on the Epistles of St. Paul. This manuscript was made at Winchcomb Abbey in Gloucestershire in the second quarter of the twelfth century.

To add beauty to manuscripts in the Middle Ages, artists decorated them with miniatures, embellished the capital letters with gold leaf and brilliant pigments, and wove borders around the page with incredible detail. Gold leaf was applied to illumine a manuscript page, giving rise to the term "illuminated manuscript."

One of the finest illuminated manuscripts in the Huntington collections is the Ellesmere manuscript of Geoffrey Chaucer's *Canterbury Tales* (c. 1410). Written on vellum, the manuscript is elaborately decorated with portraits of the twenty-three pilgrims, including one thought to be a likeness of Chaucer himself. Its fame rests not only on its handsome presentation — it is one of the best-preserved English literary manuscripts in existence — but also on the importance of its text. The Ellesmere manuscript is the earliest complete copy of Chaucer's original text, made within a decade or so of the poet's death.

"The Flight into Egypt," miniature from a Flemish manuscript Book of Hours produced toward the end of the fifteenth century.

The Ellesmere Chaucer is in excellent condition partly because it remained undisturbed in the library of Sir Thomas Egerton and his family from the early seventeenth century until Mr. Huntington purchased the collection in 1917. The handsome binding is not original but dates from the nineteenth century.

The most influential English poem of the Middle Ages apart from Chaucer's *Canterbury Tales* is William Langland's *Piers Plowman*, a visionary poem written in the last quarter of the fourteenth century which explores religious and social issues of the time. The Huntington holds four early manuscript versions.

"The Coronation of the Virgin," miniature from a French manuscript Book of Hours produced in the workshop of the Master of the Duke of Bedford in the mid-fifteenth century.

Books of Hours are among the most striking examples of illuminated manuscripts. These beautifully decorated manuscript books, used by wealthy patrons in their private chapels, contain prayers appropriate to the various canonical hours. The pages (or leaves) of such books were made of vellum, the text lettered by a scribe, the ornamental borders drawn by a specialist in decoration, and the miniature pictures painted by a master artist.

The Library frequently displays leaves from the manuscript Book of Hours illuminated by Simon Marmion between 1450 and 1475, one of the finest of the seventy-four Books of Hours in the collection.

One of the most important medieval documents in the Library's collection is a very early copy of the Magna Carta, the cornerstone of law in English-speaking countries. Manuscripts of all the statutes passed by medieval English parliaments often begin, as does the Huntington's fourteenth-century copy on parchment, with a restatement of the Magna Carta.

"The Crucifixion," miniature from a French manuscript Book of Hours illuminated by Simon Marmion in the second half of the fifteenth century.

The bindings of the Huntington volumes, stamped calfskin covering heavy oak boards, are unusual in that they also date from the fifteenth century and are a splendid example of period craftsmanship.

About 1473-74, some twenty years after the appearance of Gutenberg's printed Bible, William Caxton, mercer, diplomat, and scholar, printed his English translation of Raoul le Fevre's *Le Recueil des Histoires de Troye*. A gathering of stories about the Trojan War, this was the first book printed in the English language. Caxton also was the first to print an edition of Chaucer's *Canterbury Tales*. In all, the Huntington has thirty-three of about a hundred works from Caxton's press.

An early printing shop in an engraving by Jan van der Straet, called Stradanus, from *Nova Reperta* (prob. 1600).

The Huntington also holds and often displays fifteenth-century editions of Aristotle, Pliny, Euclid, and Dante, important for their influence on the course of intellectual history in the Renaissance and handsome in their craftsmanship.

This unique engraved frontispiece from the Huntington copy of the first book printed in English, Caxton's *History of Troy,* is believed to show Caxton presenting the book to his patroness, Margaret, Duchess of Burgundy.

The Gutenberg Bible and Early Printing

The Library's collection of more than 5,400 incunabula (books printed before 1501) is the second largest in the United States, after the Library of Congress. It includes all fields of thought of the period and, with examples from the first and principal presses of the time, it illustrates the development of the art of printing during the first half-century of its existence in Europe.

The earliest book in the collection is the Gutenberg Bible, the first substantial book printed with movable type in Europe. Printed about 1450-55, it is identified with Johannes Gutenberg (c. 1400-68) of Mainz, Germany, regarded as the inventor of printing in the West. The two-volume text is in Latin, in a version known as the Vulgate.

Only the text, in type called black-letter, or gothic, was printed with movable type. The chapter headings in red, the red and blue initials, and the large illuminated initials and marginal decorations were added by hand after the sheets were printed.

The Huntington copy is one of twelve surviving copies printed on vellum, and one of three vellum copies in America. Thirty-six copies printed on paper also survive. Thus a total of forty-eight copies still exist out of an estimated printing of 160 to 180.

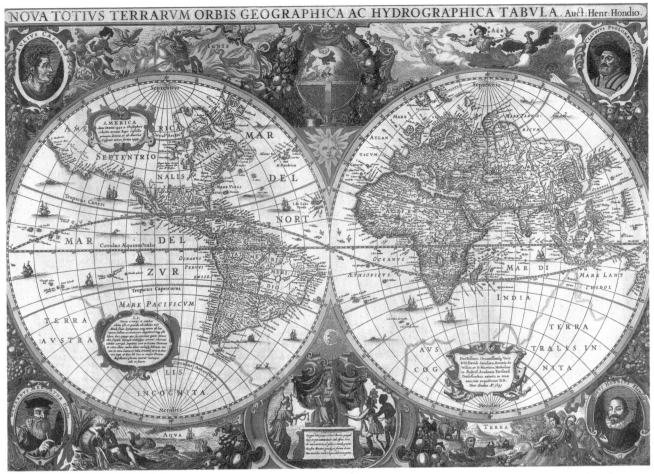

Frontispiece to a 1630 revision of the Mercator/Hondius atlas. The baroque decoration of this map includes portraits of cartographers Claudius Ptolemy, Gerard Mercator, and Jodocus Hondius, Sr.

Science and Discovery

The Renaissance in Europe was a time of geographic as well as scientific discovery. The Huntington has an important collection of fifteenth- and sixteenth-century materials on travel and exploration. Among the highlights are the King-Hamy chart of 1502, one of the first known maps to show the New World; Nicholas Vallard's magnificent illustrated atlas; and most of the early imprints of Columbus's letter describing his voyage of discovery.

The collection of works by great sixteenth- and seventeenth-century scientists represents pioneers like the Italian astronomer Galileo, botanist Leonhard Fuchs, and chemist Robert Boyle, all of whom changed conventional ways of looking at the physical world. In his *Anatomical Exercises,* William Harvey gave proof of the circulation of the blood, and Isaac Newton's *Principia* defined a system of gravitational motion that was accepted for more than two centuries.

Tycho Brahe in his observatory, from the great cartographic work of the seventeenth century, Joan Blaeu's *Grooten Atlas* (1642-65).

Some of the Library's rare early editions of Shakespeare. The First Folio of 1623 contains the first appearance in print of most of Shakespeare's plays.

William Shakespeare and the Renaissance

The sixteenth and seventeenth centuries mark the high point of English literary culture in the Renaissance. Dramatists of the age produced the greatest body of plays since Greek tragedy.

The best known, of course, was William Shakespeare (1564-1616). As an eminent writer, a successful actor and producer, and shareholder in a theatrical company, he was a remarkable man of the theater. In addition to thirty-seven plays, he wrote a sonnet cycle, two narrative poems, and shorter verses. His works have influenced profoundly the culture of all English-speaking peoples.

The Huntington collection of early Shakespeare editions remains unsurpassed by any other library in the world. Highlights include the first edition of his collected plays, known as the "First Folio." Entitled *Mr. William Shakespeare's Comedies, Histories, and Tragedies,*

the First Folio contains thirty-six plays, twenty of them printed for the first time; it is unquestionably the most important source of knowledge regarding Shakespeare's texts. The volume was compiled after Shakespeare's death by two of his theatrical associates.

The Library also holds other masterpieces produced during the period, including rare early copies of Spenser's *Faerie Queene,* Milton's *Paradise Lost,* Marvell's verse, Herbert's meditative poems, and John Bunyan's *Pilgrim's Progress,* for two centuries the most popular and influential Puritan book.

Many notable Christian books appeared during the Renaissance — among them the first Polyglot Bible, John Calvin's *Institutes,* the first printing of St. Augustine's *De civitate Dei,* the King James Bible, and the Book of Common Prayer — all in the Library's holdings.

"Romeo and Juliet," an eighteenth-century illustration from the Turner Shakespeare.

English Literature, Eighteenth to Twentieth Centuries

The Huntington's manuscripts and first editions from this period include works by some of Britain's most celebrated poets and novelists, such as Alexander Pope, Jonathan Swift, Robert Burns, Henry Fielding, William Blake, William Wordsworth, Percy Bysshe Shelley, John Keats, Lord Byron, Charles Dickens, William Makepeace Thackeray, Anthony Trollope, William Butler Yeats, and James Joyce. Letters and other writings by a large number of English literary figures may be found. To mention a few: Dickens is represented by nearly 1,000 letters; Shelley by notebooks with characteristic sketches, experimental rhymes, and bits of verse later incorporated into his poems; Robert Louis Stevenson by the journals of his voyages to the South Seas and California; and Tennyson by many poems, including part of *In Memoriam*.

One of Mr. Huntington's earliest acquisitions was a set of publications from the Kelmscott Press of William Morris, the noted poet, designer, and printer of the late nineteenth century.

Charles Dickens in 1867
(photograph by J. and B. Gurney)

Woodcut by Edward Burne-Jones for the prologue to *The Canterbury Tales*, from William Morris's Kelmscott *Chaucer* (1896).

as a Virginia plantation owner gloomy about troubles over slavery, and as an inventor of a copying machine (a reduced-scale replica is frequently on display).

Other early American materials range from Captain John Smith's first account of Virginia (1624) to George Mason's annotated draft of the U.S. Constitution (1787). Documents that influenced the American Revolution and publications of the new Republic include John Locke's *Two Treatises of Government* (1690), Thomas Paine's *Common Sense* (1776), and George Washington's first inaugural address (1789).

The Founding Fathers and American History

The development of America is well documented in the Huntington collections, with a special concentration on Revolutionary, Civil War, and western history.

The Huntington has the largest collection of letters, documents, and papers of the Founding Fathers located outside the great east coast repositories. One of the most notable of these is the manuscript of Benjamin Franklin's autobiography. Franklin began his "Memoirs," as he called them, at age sixty-five to tell the story of his life to his son and to give his own explanation of his success. He wrote in long columns on half of each side of large sheets of paper, reserving the blank half of the page for additions and corrections. More than just an account of Franklin's life, the autobiography has become an important part of America's literary heritage.

George Washington's genealogy is written in the first president's own handwriting (1792). Letters to statesmen, his officers, and family members, along with other papers, document Washington's career as the general of the Revolutionary army, his postwar inclination to retire to private life, and then his service as the first president of his country. These manuscript materials also reveal the private person, his passion for owning land, and his exercise of family responsibilities.

Thomas Jefferson's letters and printed works detail his activities as a political philosopher and a social scientist, as a statesman who brought about the Louisiana Purchase, as a patron of education and a natural scientist,

George Washington, attributed to Charles Willson Peale (1741-1827).

Battle of Franklin, November 30, 1864. One of a series of thirty-six chromolithographs of Civil War battle scenes based on Louis Kurz's wartime drawings, issued by the firm of Kurz and Allison between 1884 and 1894.

Lincoln and the Civil War

Mr. Huntington had a deep interest in Robert E. Lee and a deeper interest in Abraham Lincoln. He acquired a fine set of early Lee letters written to his wife Molly and a later series written to his favorite cousin, Martha Williams. The Lincoln collection includes more than 200 letters and manuscripts by the sixteenth President. Associated with the Lincoln collection are the let-

ters, books, and documents of Civil War nurse Clara Barton and of Civil War soldiers and their families. These provide invaluable pictures of the American experience during the Civil War (1861-65).

Letter from Lincoln, dated April 30, 1864, authorizing General Ulysses S. Grant to conduct the campaign which was the last of the Civil War.

Abraham Lincoln, detail from a photograph by Alexander Hesler (1860).

Great White Heron from the double elephant folio *The Birds of America* (1827-28) by John James Audubon.

Exploration of the New Country

In the nineteenth century, the frontier experience deeply affected American thought and feeling. Karl Bodmer, J. Goldsborough Bruff, George Catlin, and other travelers explored a new and intensely exciting continent and pictured their findings for the world.

One of the monumental works in this field is John James Audubon's famous *Birds of America*. For its commanding size, vividness of depiction, and scientific accuracy, it is an unparalleled publication. Audubon's original goal was to draw every American bird from nature in its actual size. He employed Robert Havell, Jr., in London to engrave and color the plates. Audubon published the work himself, issuing engravings to subscribers in sets of five. His intention was to bind each 100 engravings into a massive folio volume, called a double elephant folio. There turned out to be 435 plates, and their binding required four huge volumes, each weighing nearly forty-six pounds and measuring over two-and-a-half feet wide by three-and-a-half feet tall.

Bison-Dance of the Mandan Indians, hand-colored engraving with aquatint by Karl Bodmer (1809-93) for Maximilian, Prince of Wied's *Travels in the Interior of North America* (1844).

California History and Literature

Mr. Huntington paid comparatively little attention to acquiring California materials; however, his purchases laid the foundation for a remarkable collection in this field. Among the literary manuscript collections are the writings and correspondence of such figures as Ambrose Bierce, Bret Harte, Joaquin Miller, John Muir, George Sterling, Ina Coolbrith, and Mary Austin. These collections have been built upon or acquired since Mr. Huntington's death.

The Huntington possesses Jack London's manuscripts, correspondence, scrapbooks, photographs, and first editions, as well as his personal library. Numbering some 30,000 items, the collection contains the manuscripts of almost all of his works — even the charred pages of the manuscript of *The Sea Wolf*, which burned in the fire after the 1906 San Francisco earthquake.

Materials on the exploration and settlement of Spanish California include letters of Father Eusebio Kino and a copy of the diary of Juan Bautista de Anza. The Mexican War, which ended in 1848, and the Gold Rush of 1849 brought radical changes to the California of Spanish and Mexican settlement. Items from this period include a letter from John Sutter to a prospective investor telling about the discovery of gold at his mill, manuscript drafts in English and Spanish of California's constitution, and the papers of pioneers such as Abel Stearns, ranch owner and businessman of early Los Angeles.

61

Jack London, about 1900.

Sutter's Fort (1849), watercolor by John Hovey.

"Boats attacking Whales," W. J. Linton's wood-engraved frontispiece for Thomas Beale's *Natural History of the Sperm Whale* (1839).
Melville praised this illustration in his novel *Moby Dick* as "admirably correct and lifelike."

American Literature

The Library holds most of the early editions of American writers of consequence before 1900, and it also has important holdings of the works of major twentieth-century American authors, such as Conrad Aiken and Wallace Stevens.

The collection of 45,000 manuscripts, and many rare printed books, includes the manuscript and proof sheets of Henry David Thoreau's *Walden*, Edgar Allan Poe's first book of poems, composed when he was fourteen (now the rarest of his works), poems by Walt Whitman, the manuscript of Mark Twain's *The Prince and the Pauper*, and first editions of many classics of American literature, such as Herman Melville's *Moby Dick* and Mark Twain's *The Adventures of Huckleberry Finn*.

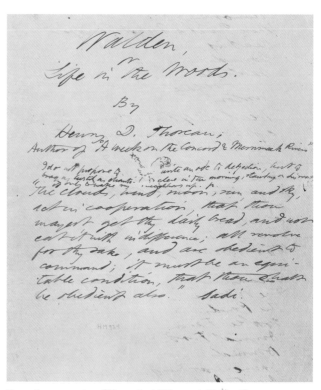

From the manuscript of Henry David Thoreau's *Walden*. Thoreau spent about six years writing this work before its publication in 1854.

Two distinguished American poets,
Robert Frost (left) and Wallace Stevens, in 1935.

The Huntington's extensive collection of early and interesting editions of American writers
includes works by Nathaniel Hawthorne, Mark Twain, and Stephen Crane.

Book and Manuscript Conservation

In the Avery Conservation Center special attention is given to the Library's rare books and manuscripts, with the goal of preserving them for a long future of use by scholars and for public display.

In the Book Conservation Laboratory, books are repaired and rebound, with first priority given to those that are most fragile or most in demand by scholars. Books printed in England between 1475 and 1640 are heavily used and thus are constantly watched for signs of disrepair. As far as possible, books are repaired and rebound in the style in which they were originally issued, and former ownership notes or marks are carefully preserved.

Manuscripts from the last hundred years or so in fact need more attention than the oldest ones. The paper of recent documents is made from wood fiber with an acidic sizing that turns it brittle; such papers need to be treated to survive. This poor-quality paper contrasts with the vellum (the treated skin of a small animal) used for medieval manuscripts and the rag used to make early paper; both of these materials are strong and durable.

In the paper conservation laboratory, damaged and defective manuscripts are given new life. Some fragile documents are encapsulated in mylar. This is a process which, like all conservation procedures, is reversible. Inside a protective covering the manuscripts can be studied by scholars with much less risk of further damage. Manuscripts are stored in the best possible conditions so they will not deteriorate; the stacks are kept at a constant temperature of sixty-eight degrees and a relative humidity of fifty percent, and these levels are continually checked. As the technology for conservation improves, the hope is that documents may be repaired using as yet undiscovered methods of restoration.

Avery Conservation Center.

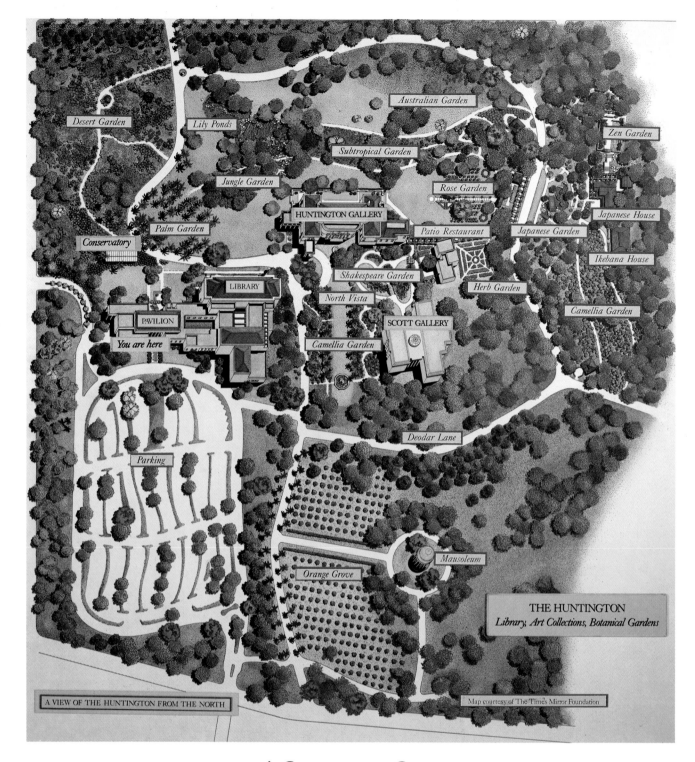

A VIEW OF THE HUNTINGTON FROM THE NORTH

Map courtesy of The Times Mirror Foundation

THE HUNTINGTON
Library, Art Collections, Botanical Gardens

A CALENDAR OF COLOR

January
Art Gallery: Kaffirboom Coral Tree, Pink Ball Dombeya
Australian: Bailey Acacia
Desert: Aloes
Japanese: Japanese Flowering Apricot
North Vista: Japonica and Sasanqua Camellias
Rose Garden: Asiatic Magnolias
Shakespeare: Iceland Poppies

February
Art Gallery: Pink Ball Dombeya
Australian: Bailey Acacia
Camellia Gardens: Reticulata and Japonica Camellias
Desert: Aloes, Euphorbias, Mesembryanthemums
Japanese: Japanese Flowering Apricot, Azaleas, Flowering
    Peaches, Formosan Cherry, Magnolias, Michelia doltsopa
North Vista: Azaleas, Reticulata and Japonica Camellias